How to Love
Someone You Can't Stand

Milton Jones

HEARTSPRING PUBLISHING · JOPLIN, MISSOURI

Cover Design by Mark A. Cole
International Standard Book Number 978-0-89900-713-7

CONTENTS

ACKNOWLEDGMENTS

Thank you, Barbie, for always being beside me and encouraging me to counsel countless numbers of people who weren't getting along. Thanks again for proofing this manuscript.

My thanks go out to my friend, Rick Atchley, for naming this book.

If imitation is the sincerest form of flattery, there are several people I have flattered in this book. Many of these ideas have been gleaned and borrowed from others. I especially owe the Christian Counseling and Educational Foundation in Laverock, Pennsylvania. All of the principles in this book were learned there. Their teaching on how to heal broken relationships was taught so well and was so pertinent that it was instantly put into practice in my ministry. Over the years, the counsel that I learned there has been repeated so often that I have long since forgotten what words belonged to my teachers and which ones were my own. Forgive me if I have stolen too many of yours. I guess you will have to continue doing good to overcome my injustice.

Two books have already been written on this topic that more than adequately cover the subject. *How to Overcome Evil* by Jay Adams and *Bold Love* by Dan Allender and Tremper Longman III. These books have greatly influenced my views in overcoming bad relationships. With two such good books, I hardly need to add another one. But my hope is that a new book might find a new audience, and these principles might once again work to restore another relationship.

I dedicate this book to my Dad,
Jimmie Jones,
who taught me how to like people.

STUDIES FOR SMALL GROUPS

Welcome to the *Studies for Small Groups* series from College Press. This series is designed for simplicity of use while giving insight into important issues of the Christian life. Some are topical studies, while others examine a passage of Scripture for the day-to-day lessons we can learn from it. The present study is a bit of both, using Romans 12:14-21 as a textual basis for a generally topical study.

A number of possible uses could be made of this study Because there are a limited number of lessons, the format is ideal for new or potential Christians who can begin the study without feeling that they are tied into an overly long commitment. It could also be used for one or two months of weekly studies by a home Bible study group. The series is suitable for individual as well as group study.

Of course, any study is only as good as the effort you put into it. The group leader should study each lesson carefully before the group study session, and if possible, come up with additional Scriptures and other supporting material. Although study questions are provided for each lesson, it would also be helpful if the leader can add his or her own questions.

Neither is it necessary to complete a full lesson in one class period. If the discussion is going well, don't feel that you have to cut it off to fit time constraints, as long as the discussion is related to the topic and not off on side issues.

If love is the greatest commandment, then how to obey that command when we find it hardest to do so is probably one of the most important studies you or your group will ever tackle. We hope this book, *How to Love Someone You Can't Stand,* will help.

HOW TO LOVE SOMEONE YOU CAN'T STAND

In fictional Seattle when people have problems, they call Dr. Frasier Crane. If you watch Frasier on television, you will notice that most of his callers have problems getting along with someone else. In real life Seattle, many people with problems call me. And just like it is with Frasier, help is needed because they are not getting along with somebody.

The majority of the time when a person ends up in my office for counseling, it is because of a bad relationship. Virtually all of the time they feel they were done wrong. It is the old "somebody done somebody wrong song," and they perceive themselves to be the victim. At one time, perhaps, they were close to this person. It could even have been their spouse. But now — they can't stand this person who has done them wrong.

How do you love somebody you can't stand?

Maybe the last thing in the world that you feel like doing is loving someone who hurt you. But Jesus tells us to love even our enemies. So how do you love somebody you can't stand?

Reflecting on countless counseling situations dealing with bad relationships, I have found one passage of Scripture to be the most helpful and the one I have used most frequently in these situations. It is probably the most radical passage on relationships, and the one least practiced. But I never have found a better one. This teaching on overcoming a bad relationship is found in Romans 12:14-21.

[14]Bless those who persecute you; bless and do not curse. [15]Rejoice with those who rejoice; mourn with those who mourn. [16]Live in harmony with one another. Do not be proud, but be willing to associate with people of low position. Do not be conceited.

[17]Do not repay anyone evil for evil. Be careful to do what is right in the eyes of everybody. [18]If it is possible, as far as it depends on you, live at peace with everyone. [19]Do not take revenge, my friends, but leave room for God's wrath, for it is written: "It is mine to avenge; I will repay,"[a] says the Lord. [20]On the contrary:

"If your enemy is hungry, feed him;

if he is thirsty, give him something to drink.

In doing this, you will heap burning coals on his head."[b]

[21]Do not be overcome by evil, but overcome evil with good.

[a]19 Deut. 32:35   [b]20 Prov. 25:21,22

Most of us believe that God can give us the power to overcome a bad relationship, but few of us seem to know the plan. The plan is found here in this section of Romans. If you have someone whom you can't stand, here are seven steps for overcoming this bad relationship. They are radical and rarely practiced. But if you want to trek on some new ground and boldly go where your relationship has never been before, I promise these steps will work.

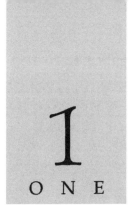

1
O N E

PEOPLE AREN'T YOUR PROBLEM

Have you ever had one of those days when it seemed like everyone in the world was bugging you? I had one a few years ago. I was upset and felt like there was no one who could understand my dilemma. I literally couldn't stand anybody. Have you ever been there?

Now normally I could talk to someone at church. But in this case the people at church were bothering me more than anyone else. And in most circumstances I have a network of friends in my religious movement who can help me. But this time I thought everyone in my movement had caused my problem. I was mad and didn't know where to turn.

Since one of my old seminary professors was in town, I decided that he should be the recipient of my wrath. He met me at a restaurant and kindly listened to me expound on my perceived injustices. After an hour of my griping he had reached his limit and said, "Milton, will you please open your Bible." I hate it when people do that to me. It's supposed to be *my* job!

He said, "Turn to Ephesians 6. Start reading in verse 12."

I began, "For our struggle is not against flesh and blood . . ."

"Stop!" he said. "Milton, after listening to you grumble, anyone would think that your struggle is against flesh and blood. You have whined about people for some time, and the Bible tells us that *people* are not our problem. No, God gave you people to minister to. If you are going to make it in ministry, or life for that matter, you had better identify your enemy. . . . Continue your reading."

I started again . . . "but against the rulers, against the authorities, against the powers of this dark world and against the spiritual forces of evil in the heavenly realms."

"There you have it!" he said. *"Your problem is not with people. It is with evil."*

SEEING THE EVIL INSTEAD OF THE PERSON

Is there someone in your life whom you can't stand? Although it may seem like they are your big problem, my old professor was correct — people are not your problem. Evil is your problem according to Paul in Ephesians 6.

Certainly, there is evil everywhere in this world. We tend to picture evil as something out of a horror movie. But usually evil is expressed in a much more subtle context. In fact, it is most often found in the context of someone you know who continues to sin against you. In this book, we are going to be examining that particular kind of evil that is directed toward you. Even though people are not your problem, Satan can use a bad relationship to tempt you to sin. That person whom you can't stand, whether he realizes it or not, can be utilized by the evil one in a spiritual battle.

Your problem is not with people. It is with evil.

10

Now most of the time this happens through unbelievers. But evil can also be done by believers. I know because I have seen evil done too often in the church. A brother in the Lord can sin against another brother. Remember Peter's question in Matthew 18: "Lord, how many times shall I forgive my brother when he sins against me? Up to seven times?" (v. 21). *Perhaps Satan's sweetest victories are when those of us in the body of Christ sin against each other.*

> Perhaps Satan's sweetest victories are when those of us in the body of Christ sin against each other.

Paul is informing us that we are in a spiritual battle between good and evil. In other words, there is a whole spiritual realm that you cannot see which is having a huge effect on your bad relationship. There is no greater battle. You are waging war against sin everywhere you go. And Satan is going to try to use people to defeat you.

If you have decided to follow in the steps of Jesus, you are going to be attacked. The goal will be to defeat you, but you don't have to lose out. The evil done to you can be overcome. In fact, you are commanded to win this conflict.

"Do not be overcome by evil, but overcome evil with good" (Romans 12:21).

In this verse, we find the key to dealing with evil in our relationships.

PROBLEMS COME FROM RELATIONSHIPS

As I reflect on many years of counseling, the majority of people's perceived problems stem from not getting along with someone else. It may have been a spouse, parent, child, friend, roommate, coworker, boss, or church member. But the conflict starts eating at them. Then, they start getting emotionally upset. And from their point of view, they feel like they have been wronged. When this is the case, Romans 12:21 is God's prescription.

This counsel may be different from what you have been told in the past. You may not want to do it once you have grasped it. But it is still what God says. And believe me, it is probably the most practical counsel you will ever hear. In this book you will learn seven steps based on Romans 12:14-21 to teach you how to overcome a bad relationship.

Because this teaching is so revolutionary and radical, we are going to study these verses in depth. But to understand these verses, it is necessary to start with the theme verse which is located at the end, and then go back to the beginning.

"Do not be overcome by evil, but overcome evil with good" (Romans 12:21).

If there is any doubt about the possibility of winning over evil, Paul wants to clear it up in Romans 12:21. God doesn't want us to merely "hold our own" when someone harms us. No, He wants us to be victorious! The struggles we face in life can actually be beneficial for us. They can be occasions for our faith to develop. If this were not the case, God wouldn't allow these wrongdoings to come our way. According to Romans 5, Christian maturity doesn't happen automatically. Instead, it is a process that begins with suffering. Notice how Paul describes the progression of our faith:

"Not only so, but we also rejoice in our sufferings, because we know that suffering produces perseverance; perseverance, character; and character, hope. And hope does not disappoint us, because God has poured out his love into our hearts by the Holy Spirit, whom he has given us" (Romans 5:3-5).

Theme Verse:
Do not be overcome by evil, but overcome evil with good

GOD SPECIALIZES IN HEALING BAD RELATIONSHIPS

Andrae Crouch stated this idea well in his song, *Through It All.* He sang "If I had never had a problem, I would have never known that God could solve them." *Problems, even bad relationships, are not to ruin us but to make us mature through a dependence on the Lord.*

> Problems, even bad relationships, are not to ruin us but to make us mature through a dependence on the Lord.

As a result, the goal for this book is to get rid of any defeatist attitudes. God can solve your problems. He has not only given you the strength to win over your strife; He has also given you a strategy. Too many Christians believe in the power of God but still don't know what to do about their problems. That's why God gives this text. So if you feel defeated, don't give up. If someone has treated you poorly, God has a strategy. And it will work.

If we are living in a sinful world, we shouldn't be astonished when people wrong us. Most of us are aware of Romans 3:23: "for all have sinned and fall short of the glory of God." If that is true, then you should count on having conflicts. And who is going to mistreat you? If all have sinned, then no one will be exempt from harming you.

On the wall of my office is a plaque with one of my favorite sayings: "The real test in golf and in life is not keeping out of the rough, but in getting out after we are in."

Heeding this advice by John Moore would not only be healthy for our golf but also for our faith. Far too often we try to live our lives where we will never have to face any rough times. That would be nice, but it is not the way life happens. We should enjoy the fairways, but the real test is going to come when you get into the rough.

Can you get out when you are in deep trouble? People are going to do bad things to you. It is unavoidable. What, therefore, is going to be your response? How are you going to get out? Can you still win if you are in the rough? Absolutely.

To overcome means to win. And Paul tells us how to win — "overcome evil with good" (Romans 12:21).

Paul is not prescribing passivity in this world. He is teaching us about aggressive discipleship. This may sound strange in light of Jesus' teaching about turning the other cheek. But *purposefully turning the other cheek is an extremely assertive action.* Jesus is not describing a situation where someone is pounding on your face because you can't do anything about it. No, he is talking about turning the other cheek when it is your choice.

This is what Jesus did. His enemies didn't take his life. We are told that he laid down his life. "This is how we know what love is: Jesus Christ laid down his life for us. And we ought to lay down our lives for our brothers" (1 John 3:16). Laying down your life is an aggressive action.

CHOOSE YOUR WEAPONS — GOOD, NOT EVIL

In every fight, you must choose your weapons. Paul also reminds us of this in Second Corinthians. "The weapons we fight with are not the weapons of the world. On the contrary, they have divine power to demolish strongholds" (2 Corinthians 10:4).

Purposefully turning the other cheek is an extremely assertive action.

The weapons of the world are evil. Our weapons are good.

If we are going to outduel the devil, we have to choose our weapons carefully. We must use godly weapons,

14

not worldly weapons. With weapons of goodness chosen, we then aggressively attack this world. When people have wronged us, we overcome their evil with our good.

You cannot use evil when something wrong has been done to you for two reasons. First of all, evil is not as powerful as good. Do you remember in the first Indiana Jones movie when he was trapped by the man with the sword? What did he do? He just pulled out his gun and shot him. It was an unfair advantage. You have a similar advantage on evil with good as your weapon.

You will always be tempted to return evil for evil. One of the reasons we do this is because we think evil is more powerful than what we possess as Christians. We need to remember John's admonition — "You, dear children, are from God and have overcome them, because the one who is in you is greater than the one who is in the world" (1 John 4:4). If you think evil is more powerful than our God, your picture of God is too small. You had better take another look at your God.

The second reason we don't return evil for evil is because *our objective is to destroy evil, not create it.* Doing evil puts you on the wrong side of God. Satan's followers are masters of evil. Do you really want to play on *his* battlefield, against *his* experts with *his* weapons? I don't think so. If we start using evil against evil as Christians, we are playing Satan's game by his rules.

So what is our response to the evil in this world? We are to do something good. Our church once received a negative accusation from a critic. He said, "You are just a bunch of do-gooders." But he was right. Christians are a bunch of do-gooders.

RESPOND WITH AGGRESSIVE GOOD

As disciples of Jesus, we are to be spokesmen against the evil in this world. But that is not enough. It is one thing to say we ought to help the homeless. It is another to do something. We have heard of all the atrocities in Calcutta. We have seen the starvation, sickness, and dead bodies. But what has had the most impact on changing that situation? Has it been the politicians and preachers that have talked about it or what that one woman, Mother Teresa, has done there?

We must do good in any evil situation. It doesn't matter how great the odds are. No matter how bad the situation is, we must respond to it aggressively with good.

As I walked into Room 306 at the Lorraine Motel in Memphis, I could hear his words. Although they were spoken in 1968, his words were no less convicting. Standing in the room near where Martin Luther King, Jr. was shot and hearing him speak of going to the mountaintop had a haunting effect. His famous speech is played continually at the National Civil Rights Museum. But as I listened, I only wished people could have heard the rest of the sermon.

I'm afraid that too many today want to share his dream of unity and harmony but simply don't know how. Dr. King told us how to do it earlier in his sermon as he expounded on a biblical text. The plan for accomplishing the dream was by doing good.

His text in that sermon was the Parable of the Good Samaritan.

> To do good may require a loss of time, money, position, and pride.

And from this momentous sermon, Dr. King helped me to see the questions that mark not only the differences in the Good Samaritan and the priests and Levite, but also the differences between doing good and evil. Certainly, this story paints a picture of people who were enemies. The Samaritans and Jews had been wronging each other for years. In fact, they couldn't stand each other.

What is going to happen to this world if we don't do good?

ASK THE RIGHT QUESTION

King stated that the question that the Levite and priest asked when they saw the needy man on the side of the road was, "What will happen to me if I help this person?" It was not an aggressive evil. It was merely a passive evil or a lack of an aggressive good. They just didn't get involved because it demanded something of them.

To do good may require a loss of time, money, position, and pride. Religious and racial hassles can also occur if the person is not like us. We see a lot of this kind of evil, don't we? "What will happen to me if I help this person?" This question is at the very root of why we don't want to do good to the person who wronged us.

The Samaritan is good because he finally asks the right question: "What will happen to *him* if I don't help?" And then he gives his assistance to the very kind of person he most likely can't stand. *Good is when you get your focus off yourself and look at someone else (even if that someone is a person you can't stand).* Then, if you are good, you see their needs and do something about them.

What is going to happen to this world if we don't do good? Think about it. This world is lost. Truly, we are wronged by the injustices of this world everyday. But what is going to happen to people if we don't help? Can we decide that we just can't stand the world and with indifference let it go to hell?

What is going to happen to the church if we don't do good? Churches today are being plagued with divisions that are usually started because we wrong each other. What is going to happen to the church if we don't quit this? What is going to happen if we don't start serving our brothers and sisters, even the ones that we can't stand because of what they have done? How can we overcome the evil in this world with good when we haven't even learned to do it in the church?

Jesus is the supreme example of doing good, isn't He?

He asks, "What will happen to them if I don't help?" That is ultimately what Jesus asked when we had wronged Him. And the answer is that we would be lost. And so good fought evil. And the cross was the ultimate evil. The cross is all the evil the world could throw out. And we proclaim Jesus today because good overcame the evil. Because He conquered, there is also victory for you.

"Do not be overcome by evil, but overcome evil with good."

Good is when you get your focus off yourself and look at someone else (even if that someone is a person you can't stand).

18

REFLECTING ON LESSON ONE

1. What situations have made you feel like people were your problem?

2. What is the root of our problems with people? How would you define "evil"?

3. Have most of your emotional struggles been because of bad relationships? If so, what kinds of relationships have been the source of your anxiety?

4. What is the key teaching in the Bible for overcoming bad relationships?

5. How is suffering in relationships actually a part of the progression of our faith?

6. How is "overcoming evil with good" an aggressive action rather than a passive principle?

7. What are the weapons Christians use in overcoming evil? What problems occur when they render evil for evil?

8. What questions did Martin Luther King, Jr. use to differentiate between doing good and evil? How was Jesus an example of answering the right question?

9. Where are some places in the world and at church that you need to do good in your relationships?

2
T W O

TALK ISN'T CHEAP

For three and a half years, Jeri Boley of Canby, Oregon had hoped that justice would prevail and her son's killer would bear the consequences of his horrible crime.

Brian, her twenty-year-old son, had been riding his motorcycle home from work when a drunken driver, Ruben Gonzalez, ran over him. After the ordeal of a three-and-a-half-year wait, the sentencing was finally going to occur, or was it?

On the day before the sentencing, her legal advocate revealed some complications because of a newborn sympathy toward Mr. Gonzalez. The court had begun to feel sorry for Ruben because of his son's heart condition. Jeri was told that they could delay the entire legal process because his son was only expected to live for another six months.

"Every day since Brian's death, I had fought a battle in my heart against a bitter thirst for vengeance," Jeri said. "Yet I also believed that the man who had snuffed out my beautiful son's life should be punished. It might teach others a lesson about drinking and driving. All I want is justice."

"Of course I felt bad," she added, "for the dying boy who was also named Bryan. But I had lost my own son. I wasn't given a chance to say good-bye. Brian had been killed instantly when Gonzalez's vehicle struck him head-on."

The next day in the courtroom Jeri was to read an emotional statement about her son and his death. In her evening prayers, she asked God to give her strength to make it through the next day. At the very moment she was uttering this prayer, her husband walked in and said, "Jeri, we've got to leave justice to God."

As a result, she concluded her prayer, "Father, please give us the strength to accept whatever the judge decides tomorrow as an expression of your will."

The next day she read her compelling and emotional statement. In conclusion, Jeri said, "Finally I pray that God will be merciful and let your boy Bryan live. But if you lose him, you will know the devastation we have known losing our Brian."

The judge wasted no time and sentenced Ruben Gonzalez to prison immediately. Knowing she finally had her justice still did not release Jeri from her pain. As a result, she decided that the best thing to do was to tell Gonzalez that she forgave him. *But on the inside, Jeri didn't even come close to feeling like forgiving him.* Denying her feelings, she went up behind Gonzalez, put her arm on his back and said, "I want you to know that I forgive you, and we will be praying for your son.

The wall was torn down. Gonzalez burst into tears and said, "I am so sorry.

Finally, it was over, or so it seemed. When Jeri got home,

the ache was still there. Where was peace to be found? After some agonizing prayer, Jeri went to her husband and said, "I know this sounds strange after all we have been through, but I feel very strongly that we should ask the court to let Mr. Gonzalez be with his son.

The Boleys were certain that it was too late to change the sentence, but they were determined to try. The next day when they went to the court, upon the request of Jeri Boley, the court decided to let Mr. Gonzalez be with his dying son while he was still alive.

After the sentencing, Ruben Gonzalez' sister surprised Jeri by introducing her to an extremely elated little boy. She introduced Jeri to Bryan. Bryan thanked her for giving his daddy back to him.

Jeri said that as she stroked the little boy's head and offered a prayer of thanksgiving in her heart, she was finally able to say to her own son, "Good-bye, Brian."

On that day Jeri Boley was not overcome by evil but had overcome evil with good. This is the key to loving people we can't stand. It is the essence of overcoming bad relationships.

"Do not be overcome by evil, but overcome evil with good" (Romans 12:21).

How does overcoming evil with good happen? Let's look at step #1.

STEP #1: MANAGE YOUR MOUTH — BLESS AND DON'T CURSE.

Discipleship involves walking in the steps of Jesus. But *you can't walk right if you can't talk right.* Paul begins his teaching on overcoming bad relationships by stating — "Bless those who persecute you; bless and do not curse" (Romans 12:14).

You can't walk right if you can't talk right.

22

The point of this passage is to identi-fy the proper response when some-one wrongs you. What are you sup-posed to do when you have a bad relationship? Many of us consider ourselves to have a degree of spiri-tual maturity. In other words, we have learned to control our actions. When someone wrongs us, generally we don't practice immediate physical and punitive retribution. If someone gossips about us, we don't punch them out. We are far too mature to order a drive-by shooting simply because someone treated us poorly. But what do you *say* when it happens? Evil can be verbal, not just physical.

What kind of relationship is Paul talking about here in verse 14 when it says that you are persecuted? And note it well — it doesn't say "if you are persecuted." There is a promise in Second Timothy that most of us would rather not claim: "In fact, everyone who wants to live a godly life in Christ Jesus will be persecuted" (2 Timothy 3:12). So what should you be envisioning as persecu-tion?

Do you know where you are wronged most frequently? It happens in the family. Then at work. And with friends. And sometimes even at church.

And when persecution happens, I promise that your first inclination will be to say something derogatory about the person who wronged you. If an argument ensues, you will want to win it. And if you do win the argument, it is still possible that you will lose the rela-tionship. We overcome or win by good — not evil, remember?

Therefore, *the starting place for this battle is your mouth. It is the first step in winning the war.* But if you don't watch it, you will never get to the second step in overcoming a bad relationship. Most people lose the battle to Satan right here with their mouths.

WHAT IS CURSING?

Paul's whole teaching here centers around two words — bless and curse. Let's see if we can understand these words a little bit better.

Starting with the negative, what does it mean to curse? Cursing means three things. First of all, you say bad things about another person to God. You could ask God to damn them for what they did to you. "God, send them to hell, do not let them pass go or collect $200."

You will see this sentiment at certain times in the Psalms. "Let death seize upon them, and let them go down quick into hell: for wickedness is in their dwellings, and among them" (Psalm 55:15, KJV).

But most of us today aren't quite like the psalmist. In fact, *we have a tendency to avoid God altogether when it comes to bad relationships.* We simply don't talk much about it to God, unless it is a selfish complaint.

But we do talk to other people! That is the second way to curse. You say bad things about someone to other people. You could curse them. Or maybe you use a disparaging or vulgar slam. Perhaps, you get so intense that you use a profane or four-letter word. I have heard it happen, even among Christians.

On occasion, you might damn a person to someone else. But usually, you simply slander or tear them down. Whatever another person's view is of the person who wronged you, you do your best to make it lower. That is evil too, if you didn't know it. Most often, when we are wronged, we gossip about the one who wronged us.

We have a tendency to avoid God altogether when it comes to bad relationships.

24

Have you done that at work lately? How about at church?

I was listening recently to my son's CD of Weird Al Yankovich. Pat was sharing with me a song of an unrequited love where the guy felt overwhelmingly wronged that his lover was leaving him. As a result, he sang, "I would rather spend eternity eating shards of broken glass than to spend one more minute with you." In fact that was one of the milder statements he made. But haven't you felt that way before? Haven't you been that mad at someone? Did you say things that were equally as cutting?

The third way to curse is to say bad things to the person who wronged you. Like, "I'm going to get you for that." Or, "You stupid blankety-blank." You know what I am talking about, don't you? You make sure that you verbally put that person who wronged you in their place. It's your right, isn't it? Sure, but *a lot of times Christians give up their rights. That is what being a servant is all about.* Remember the deal about turning the other cheek?

WHAT IS BLESSING?

Then, what is a blessing? It is just the opposite. It is saying good about that person to God. Or at least asking for good to happen to the person who wronged you. Maybe this is the best starting place for overcoming a bad relationship. Have you ever tried it?

It is difficult to have a terrible attitude toward someone for whom you are sincerely praying. If you can honestly pray for a person, you may not change the other person, but *you* may change in the process. And sometimes you will even see your enemy change.

Isn't this what Jesus did on the cross?

"Jesus said, 'Father, forgive them, for they do not know what they are doing.' And they divided up his clothes by casting lots" (Luke 23:34).

Stephen did the same thing when they were stoning him. "Then he fell on his knees and cried out, 'Lord, do not hold this sin against them.' When he had said this, he fell asleep" (Acts 7:60).

Does God answer prayers for enemies? Look at Pentecost.

"Therefore let all Israel be assured of this: God has made this Jesus, whom you crucified, both Lord and Christ" (Acts 2:36).

Have you ever thought about this? Weren't the people who responded to God at Pentecost the answer to Jesus' prayer on the cross for those who had wronged him? And what was the answer to Stephen's prayer? Wasn't it Paul? Would Paul have been converted without Stephen's prayer? Only God knows.

Maybe the most interesting prayer for enemies is in the book of Job. Certainly you are aware of Job's misfortunes. He lost everything in that little deal that God and Satan made. And if that wasn't enough, he got persecuted for it in the form of counsel. Eliphaz, Bildad, Zophar and Elihu were all counseling him by telling him what had really caused things to go wrong. They were miserable comforters. And worst of all, they were wrong.

But have you ever noticed the part where Job had his family and fortunes restored? Look at it.

"After Job had prayed for his friends, the LORD made him prosperous again and gave him twice as much as he had before" (Job 42:10).

Blessing also means saying good things about your enemy to other people.

Job blessed the very men who had made his life miserable. When he did, God blessed Job.

26

Blessing also means saying good things about your enemy to other people. You are not to tear them down. No, you are to build them up in the sight of others. Do you do that with family members? Even the in-laws? What do you say about your boss who is unbelievably unfair? Can I assume that your words are always full of blessing for your church leaders?

To say good when evil is done seems foolish to most of us. The Proverb writer says it is foolish not to do it.

Barnabas is a good example for us in this respect. In Acts 15, Barnabas and Paul have assisted the Jerusalem conference in bringing unity to churches worldwide. No sooner is the conference over than Barnabas and Paul have such a bitter disagreement that they can no longer work together. They had brought the world together but couldn't get their own friendship together. Their controversy revolved around what Paul was saying about John Mark. Can't you hear his comments? "He is a quitter . . . He's no good in ministry . . . I will not work with him . . . He is unqualified."

But Barnabas won't say those kinds of things about John Mark. Barnabas blesses and doesn't curse. What was the result of his blessing? Well, we have the Gospel of Mark today, don't we?

To say good when evil is done seems foolish to most of us. The Proverb writer says it is foolish not to do it.

"Do not answer a fool according to his folly, or you will be like him yourself" (Proverbs 26:4).

But on the other hand, from one perspective it is foolish.

Paul said, "We are fools for Christ, but you are so wise in Christ! We are weak, but you are strong! You are honored, we are dishonored!" (1 Corinthians 4:10).

If you look at the context, what is being seen as foolish

in Corinth? It is blessing people when we are persecuted. Paul goes further in his commentary — "We work hard with our own hands. When we are cursed, we bless; when we are persecuted, we endure it; when we are slandered, we answer kindly. Up to this moment we have become the scum of the earth, the refuse of the world" (1 Corinthians 4:12-13).

Sure, the world will think you are a fool to bless people who wrong you. But they don't understand good. A man was walking down the street one day with one of those sandwich boards on his back. In the front where there is usually an advertisement was the statement, "I am a fool for Christ's sake." Perhaps it seemed comical until you read the other side of his board which said, "Whose fool are you?"

The third kind of blessing is saying something good to the person you can't stand. Now, hold it. Isn't this going too far? Yes, in fact it is downright radical.

But as Christians, we have to take our words seriously.

James tells us, "With the tongue we praise our Lord and Father, and with it we curse men, who have been made in God's likeness. Out of the same mouth come praise and cursing. My brothers, this should not be" (James 3:9-10).

Jesus put it this way, "For by thy words thou shalt be justified, and by thy words thou shalt be condemned" (Matthew 12:37, KJV).

Talk isn't cheap. When it comes to relationships, talk can make or break them.

In our conversations, we need to start listening to what we are saying. Managing our mouths is easy to understand but tough to practice. Here's the point: to overcome a bad relationship, don't talk about yourself and don't talk about other people

The third kind of blessing is saying something good to the person you can't stand.

28

negatively. Instead, talk positively about God and other people (even that one you can't stand).

REFLECTING ON LESSON TWO

1. In what places have you most often been wronged or received persecution?

2. What is usually your first inclination when someone wrongs you?

3. What does it mean to "curse" someone? Which of the three aspects of cursing poses problems for you?

4. What is a "blessing"?

5. What are some biblical examples where enemies were blessed to God? Have you ever done this? If so, what were the results?

6. Can you think of an instance where a person said good things about an enemy to someone else? What were the consequences?

7. Why does "blessing" seem so foolish to the world?

8. What does the Bible teach us about the use of our tongue?

9. Where do you need to start in managing your mouth?

3
T H R E E

WALK A MILE IN MY MOCCASINS

Will you ever be able to forget the violent scenes of Los Angeles after the not guilty verdict in the Rodney King beating case? Many stories of people battering other people were in the news, but one story escaped the attention of the media.

Gregory Alan-Williams couldn't have been in a more volatile place when Los Angeles erupted. Being African American, Gregory had been incensed by the King verdict. But it was nothing new. He was aware of the long-standing prejudice against blacks in America.

Standing at the corner of Florence and Normandie, Gregory saw cars pelted with bricks and bottles. He observed a white man being pulled from his truck and horribly beaten. Later, he witnessed another Caucasian couple as they were just about to get it. He even thought about helping them, but he didn't.

Then, an Asian man by the name of Takao Hirata drove by in a brown Ford Bronco. Bricks were hurled at the Bronco until Takao had to stop because of his broken windshield. Quickly someone crawled through the back door of Takao's vehicle and began pounding him. Gregory watched as the driver was hammered like a punching bag.

Gregory had learned the second principle of overcoming evil with good.

At that point, a thought entered Gregory's mind. Being inspired, Gregory ran over and pulled the man out of the Bronco. He begged the attackers not to hurt him. But it was too late. Takao had already been hit over the head with a bottle. He was so beat up that he could no longer walk. Realizing his need, Gregory put an arm around him. Together, they hobbled down the street.

But the violence didn't stop. As he carried Takao, another antagonist hit Takao in the face with a bottle. The vehemence happened again and again. With his arms around him, Gregory kept carrying Takao to safety.

GOD HELP US

Finally, a police car emerged containing both a white and a black policeman. Gregory pleaded for their help. They drove off without a word. That's when the ultimate words were uttered. "God help us," he said.

In a matter of moments, another African American in a Chevy van drove up and offered to help. Takao was speedily taken to safety. On April 29, 1992, Gregory Alan-Williams had saved the life of Takao Hirata.

But what was it that entered his head back on the street corner and started this heroic rescue?

"I thought back to an incident that had happened when I was a 12-year-old in Des Moines, Iowa," Gregory said. "I had just been transferred to a school where I was one of two black kids. I was coming out of the auditorium from band practice one day, carrying my clarinet, when a huge kid rushed up and punched me, splitting my lip.

I staggered back, dazed and bleeding. Later the vice-principal explained that I had held my head a little too high, and many of the students resented it. I was angry."

At that moment, Gregory's motto became "Do unto others before they do unto you." That was his rallying cry until he started going to church and learned an important principle: he was his brother's keeper.

What caused the change that had Gregory running into the streets of violence? He remembered how he had felt when he was beaten up in Des Moines. And he identified with Mr. Takao in the car. *He had learned the second principle of overcoming evil with good.*

Paul continues his teaching on overcoming bad relationships and says, "Rejoice with those who rejoice; mourn with those who mourn. Live in harmony with one another. Do not be proud, but be willing to associate with people of low position. Do not be conceited" (Romans 12:15-16).

This passage is usually examined as a topic outside of its context. This may work because these subjects are taught in other places in the Bible. But I would like to look at these verses in the context of overcoming evil with good. Romans 12:15-16 is in a context teaching us how to deal with bad relationships. Paul is still showing us how to respond when people wrong us.

Our passage here is not that different from the old Native American proverb that says. "To understand a man you must walk a mile in his moccasins." Paul has already explained that if you have a bad relationship, first of all, you manage your mouth. Secondly, he tells us to *try to see things from the other person's point of view.*

Try to see things from the other person's point of view.

32

STEP #2: PUT YOURSELF IN THE OTHER PERSON'S PLACE AND TRY TO UNDERSTAND THEIR FEELINGS, THOUGHTS AND POSITION.

> It is not a question of whether or not it was wrong. It was wrong. But why did they do it?

If someone has wronged you, it was wrong. But there may be some reasons behind it that make it more understandable. If you can identify with those reasons, you might not be so hot under the collar, and you may even be able to help. As the French philosopher, Pascal, stated, "The heart has its reasons which reason knows not of."

Stephen Covey in his national bestseller tells people how to make changes in their personal lives. He calls it *The Seven Habits of Highly Effective People.* As you read it, one of the most striking habits is "Seek First to Understand, then to be Understood."

Paul teaches this same empathetic principle as understanding a person from three different aspects.

UNDERSTAND THEIR EMOTION

"Rejoice with those who rejoice; mourn with those who mourn" (Romans 12:15).

Have you noticed that most of the times that you are hurt, it is during an emotional time? Either you are emotional and especially sensitive, or the person who hurts you is emotional and especially *in*senstive. Instead of focusing on your own emotions when someone wrongs you, try something different. If you want to have a better relationship, walk in their moccasins and see how they feel. How is this other person feeling? Don't simply judge the behavior. *It is not a question of whether or not it was wrong. It was wrong. But why did they do it?*

What are the feelings that dominate their life at that moment? Try to share those emotions.

If a person is in grief, don't you think it will govern their behavior? In the same book, Stephen Covey tells the story of getting on a subway in New York City with a man with several kids. The children were running wild. They were screaming, throwing things, and disturbing everyone around them.

What did the father do? He simply sat there and did nothing. Covey was thinking what a lousy parent this man was. He had no control over his kids. He had no sensitivity for other passengers.

Hoping that he would do something about it, Covey goes to the man and tells him how his children are misbehaving. The man responded apologetically and said he didn't even notice. He had just come from the hospital where his wife had died, and he and the kids were so overwhelmed that he was oblivious to what was happening on the subway.

It is a lot easier to understand this man's behavior when you get into his shoes, isn't it? It would be a little bit easier to have a relationship with him once you felt his pain.

One night it was bedtime and our kids were misbehaving and not wanting to go to bed (more than usual). My first thought was that I wanted to ground them for life. But their behavior became more understandable when we talked to them. Rather than yelling at them, a little discussion revealed that they were afraid to go to bed because of the scary television show we had watched earlier. Again, it was easier to have a relationship when I tried to feel the fear that they were feeling.

I have a friend that used to drive me nuts because he talked so much about himself and always tried to

> It was easier to have a relationship with him when I felt his insecurity.

position himself in the limelight at church. Gradually, I started avoiding him and began to dislike him.

I didn't really care for him until one day when I listened to his story. After listening to his tale, I found out that he was an orphan and had been passed around a lot. He was very insecure about relationships and typically ended up going overboard in personal encounters in order to get people's acceptance. *It was easier to have a relationship with him when I felt his insecurity.*

> Jesus knew weddings and funerals were vulnerable times, and that they should be shared for the sake of good relationships.

Now, what Paul is telling us here in Romans 12 is that if we want to have good relationships, we need to share the highs and lows of people's lives. We must try to capture their feelings.

"Rejoice with those who rejoice; mourn with those who mourn" (Romans 12:15).

Have you ever noticed how often Jesus was at weddings and funerals in the Gospels? Could it be that he wanted to be with people at the times when they were experiencing their greatest emotional highs and lows? I have noticed in my ministry that people nearly always remember who came to their wedding and who attended funerals of loved ones. *Jesus knew these were vulnerable times and that they should be shared for the sake of good relationships.*

Time and again we get our feelings backwards. One evening I was watching a countdown of the best television reruns of all time. The winner was a famous episode of *The Mary Tyler Moore Show* called "Chuckles the Clown." Mary Tyler Moore attended the funeral of a well-known clown named Chuckles. During the sobriety of the funeral, Mary started laughing. While most of the people attending were appalled, the minister recognized her dilemma and said it was appropriate to laugh because Chuckles had devoted his life to making people laugh. As a result, everyone in the crowd began to laugh except for Mary who then cried uncontrollably.

But here in this text, the Apostle Paul is talking about getting our feelings backwards in another way. *Frequently, we have trouble empathizing with other people's emotions.* If they are really happy and rejoicing, we get jealous.

A good example of this is in Luke 15 if you look at these three parables together. First of all, there is a lost sheep. After the shepherd finds it, he gets with all of his friends, and they are delighted. That's the appropriate emotion for the moment.

Next, a woman loses her coin. After searching and searching, it is finally recovered. With great joy coming from the moment, she throws a party. Their emotions matched the moment.

In the final story, a son is lost. Eventually, the prodigal is found. The father sets a feast. They eat the prize calf. Everyone is elated. It is the proper emotion of the moment. Then all of a sudden in the parable, something is wrong. The older brother appears, and he pouts rather than rejoices. He does not share the proper emotion of the moment.

This is the problem with relationships that go sour. You do not share the proper emotion of the moment. If everything is going wonderful for someone who has wronged you, do you rejoice or feel jealous? Do you wish grief on them, or are you happy for their good fortune? And if everything is bad and falling apart in their life, are you glad? Are you thinking that they

> Frequently, we have trouble empathizing with other people's emotions.

36

deserve their misfortune for what they did to you?

In overcoming a bad relationship, you not only need to say good instead of bad, but you also must try to share their feelings.

UNDERSTAND THEIR THINKING

Paul continues this teaching on empathy by stating, "Live in harmony with one another. Do not be proud, but be willing to associate with people of low position. Do not be conceited" (Romans 12:16).

Perhaps the message is even clearer in the King James Bible when it reads, "Be of the same mind one toward another. Mind not high things, but condescend to men of low estate. Be not wise in your own conceits" (Romans 12:16, KJV).

It is not only how a person feels that may cause a bad reaction to you. It may also be how they think. That is why Paul instructs us to have "the same mind." Here he is not talking about the mind of Christ as much as simply trying to get into that other person's brain.

What does this person think about what they are doing? We have already established that what they have done was wrong. But *what do they think about what they have done?* If they are not Christians, how can you expect them to have your value system?

An acquaintance of mine is always demanding in her relationships. She is consistently fishing for compliments to the point of belittling herself. She thinks that she is unattractive and unpopular. However, she is not. But she thinks she is, so she acts that way. In the past, she has done some very inappropriate things to be noticed, accepted, or loved. But if you knew how she

37

was put down as a child, you would understand why she has these thoughts.

To forge a better relationship with someone you can't stand, you must get into their head and try to see things as they see them. Their thoughts may be wrong and totally off base. But understanding how they see the situation is important information if you are truly interested in reconciliation.

UNDERSTAND THEIR POSITION

"Do not be proud, but be willing to associate with people of low position. Do not be conceited" (Romans 12:16).

History has been full of people putting other people down. We have a tendency to position people. And if we are not careful, we may try to position people to where they are below us. In Paul's time, there was slavery. But even when slavery doesn't exist, there will always be a group of people who are looked down upon. It can happen because of race, economic status, social position, academic background, or rank at work.

If you go down to the Central District in Seattle, you may meet an angry young gang member who will hate you instantly. In mere moments, he could wrong you. But before you write this person off of the planet, maybe you should try to understand his position. If you are not black, try to comprehend what it is like to be black in a country that still harbors a lot of prejudice. Try to realize what it is like to have no money and few prospects for a job. Try to grasp what it is like to grow up without a father's influence. Try to sense what it is like to have all your peers as gang members who are threatening you if you are not violent. Try to see things from that perspective, and maybe there will be some hope for healing.

History has been full of people putting other people down.

38

In bad relationships, we nearly always take the position of looking down at the other person. We act like we are better than they are. But we may not understand their position. I met a woman who always treated men rudely. Was that right? No. However, if you researched her history, you would find that she was abused by some men in the past. Was it fair for her to treat me poorly because of it? No. But there is a greater chance of healing and change if I try to see her position.

In bad relationships, we nearly always take the position of looking down at the other person.

In Christian circles there has been an abundance of discussion about the wrongs of radical feminism. But these extremes do not excuse men from trying to see things from a woman's position. The day men do, there will be a lot of changes in relationships in our society and in our churches.

Everyone in life has a position. In fact, we all have various positions. You may have a prestigious position at church, but a low one at work. Your education may position you at the bottom, but your popularity may rank you high socially. Most of us can figure out our own positions. We know what life is like where we live. However, we rarely analyze what it is like to be in another position in life. If you did, maybe you would recognize the motivation behind why you were wronged. It may not solve the problem, but at least the wrong will make a little more sense.

There's a lot of evil that needs to be overcome, isn't there? Will you do something about it? How do you start?

1. Manage your mouth — bless and don't curse.

2. Put yourself in the other person's place and try to understand their feelings, thoughts and position.

REFLECTING ON LESSON THREE

1. When something goes wrong in your life, do you generally seek first to understand or to be understood? Give an example.

2. Tell of a situation where someone tried to see life from another person's perspective. What was the result?

3. What are some of the emotions behind people's bad behavior that help explain their actions?

4. Where are some good places to practice "rejoicing with one another" and "mourning with one another"?

5. Have you ever had backwards emotions like the elder brother in the story of the Prodigal Son? What caused them?

6. How could someone think differently from you about a situation where evil took place?

7. How can you better understand what a person is thinking?

8. What would be a position in life that might tempt you to do bad things? Why? Do people have to react negatively simply because of their position? What does the Bible teach about where to position ourselves?

9. How can you come to know what it is like to be in a certain position?

10. Consider someone you can't stand. What are some emotions, thoughts and positioning that could cause their annoying behavior?

ALWAYS SAY NEVER

When *Forrest Gump* won the Oscar, it was unusual because it was not the typical American kind of movie. In fact, Forrest Gump was anything but the typical American hero. He was a kinder, gentler, dumber hero. He was nothing like an Arnold Schwarzenegger or Sylvester Stallone. No, the *typical* American hero was seen in the movie that won the Oscar in 1992. It was a western that had all the virtues Americans tend to think are the American way — the Clint Eastwood style of hero as seen in *Unforgiven.*

Nearly all of us have been raised on the Western movie. Time and again, the cinema has shown us a town full of innocent people who had been mistreated by horrible outlaws. Through corruption or ineptitude, the sheriff allowed the criminals to take over the streets of Dodge City, Laredo, Tombstone, or wherever. And finally, one cowboy couldn't take it anymore. He had been calm for a spell, but one high noon he decided that enough was enough. He must take the law into his own hands. So he strapped on his six-shooter. Single-handedly, the man in the white hat drew his gun, killed about twenty of the desperados and ran the rest out of town. In Hollywood we call this being a hero. If you made this kind of movie in 1992, you would get an Oscar for the best picture of the year.

God doesn't want us to go out after revenge.

And yet if you read your Bible, you will discover that this is not God's kind of hero at all. Because cleaning up the town Clint Eastwood style is what the Bible calls vengeance. And *God doesn't want us to go out after revenge.* If somebody does you wrong, don't get him back. Why? It is not your job. It's God's job.

And it is not only God's job, it is also one of His names. In the Old Testament, one of the names for God is Yah*weh Gmolah,* the Lord of Recompenses or the Lord of Vengeance.

Because of the wickedness of Babylon, Jeremiah prophesied that the Lord of Vengeance would come upon her. "A destroyer will come against Babylon; her warriors will be captured, and their bows will be broken. For the LORD is a God of retribution; he will repay in full" (Jeremiah 51:56).

Again in the Book of the Law, God declared His exclusive right to carry out revenge. "It is mine to avenge; I will repay. In due time their foot will slip; their day of disaster is near and their doom rushes upon them" (Deuteronomy 32:35).

So, according to the Bible, when are you to take revenge? Never. One of the hardest lessons to learn is that revenge is not yours. Never!!! There are no exceptions. It belongs to God so much that he wears it as His name. It is not your name.

There are a couple of mistakes that you can make about revenge.

The first mistake is that vengeance is bad. *Vengeance isn't bad. It just isn't your job.* If it was bad, then God would be bad.

Dr. Dan Allender, a Christian counselor, asked a lady what she would like to do to her husband who had just had an affair. She said, "I would like to scream at him for hours and then shoot him." Dr. Allender said, "You seem to be a little more lenient than God."

He then asked, "Would you be willing to have him lie down face-first in manure, slowly drown, and then to be trampled by a team of horses?"

"No, that's disgusting!" she replied.

"Well, in Isaiah 25:4-12, God says that's exactly what He wants to do to those who commit adultery against Him."

It is not wrong to be angry at things that are evil. It is not wrong to want justice. Revenge in its purest form is not bad. It is simply the hope that others will pay for their wrongdoings. That is good. You should hope and pray for justice. But it is just not *your job* to be the enforcer.

The second mistake is to believe that not taking revenge means total passivity. That is not at all what this passage is teaching us. God's Word doesn't instruct us to sit back and let evil walk all over us. *Letting God take care of revenge doesn't mean that we never say an action is wrong or do something about it.*

No, we are to be aggressive when it comes to evil. But we are to aggressively do good. We are just not to do evil or individually be the executors of justice.

I've seen too many Christian vigilantes. What do I mean? They take judgment into their own hands. They act like they are doing what they are doing for a noble cause, but they apparently don't understand what Paul was teaching in Romans 12.

Vengeance isn't bad. It just isn't your job.

To make sure that we don't miss the point, he says it twice. "Do not repay anyone evil for evil. Be careful to do what is right in the eyes of everybody" (Romans 12:17).

"Do not take revenge, my friends, but leave room for God's wrath, for it is written: 'It is mine to avenge; I will repay,' says the Lord" (Romans 12:19).

> Letting God take care of revenge doesn't mean that we never say an action is wrong or do something about it.

What are our steps for overcoming a bad relationship? First of all, you must manage your mouth. You bless the person that you can't stand and don't curse him. Secondly, you try to see things from the other person's point of view (his emotions, his thoughts, and his position).

And the third step comes from Romans 12:17.

STEP #3: NEVER, NEVER, NEVER TAKE REVENGE.

Did you notice that I said "Never" here? Do you know what that means? There is never a good time for you to put on the judicial robes and right the wrongs done to you. There are no loopholes in this law.

I have a friend who lost his job through other people's political maneuverings at his company. After his dismissal, however, the company realized they still needed him for a major deal that was going to cost them a lot of money without his help. I remember saying to him, "Well, I guess you got your payback now."

He said, "That is exactly why I am going to help them — because I'm not supposed to get payback."

If God is the judge, then we need to trust Him. He will take care of the situation. He sees everything. He knows everything. He is well equipped to be the judge.

Habakkuk's cry that "justice comes out perverted" certainly seems relevant in our day and age. Our legal system has failed us frequently. We worry that we will never see justice in our own lives because we witness the guilty going free everyday.

It is easy to lose our patience when it comes to justice. With long trials that border on the absurd like the one for O.J. Simpson, we tend to lose confidence in the law. It just takes too long to decide guilt. But if we are honest, it often feels like God's system of justice is taking a long time. It doesn't make sense. How long am I going to have to wait before retribution takes place? But don't get impatient. *There will be no failures in God's judicial system.* His docket may not match your own. But your impatience, in view of this verse, is really contempt of court. So don't be in such a hurry! Your day in court will come.

WHY SHOULD YOU LET GOD BE THE JUDGE?

Vengeance is not under your jurisdiction. If God wanted, He could delegate the rights of judgment and punishment to us. But He decided to keep that dominion for Himself.

God is going to take care of all restitution. Being the judge is not your calling. God knows what to do and when to do it. You can count on it. There will be a judgment. Wait for His. His judgment has been described as that final fireworks display that lights up the sky on the Fourth of July. By comparison, *your judgment will be like that little firecracker you shot off in the backyard. His will be much more spectacular.*

This person may repent. Your judgment could interfere with someone's coming to the Lord. You never know who might make an about face.

There will be no failures in God's judicial system.

46

Who would have ever dreamed that Jeffrey Dahmer, the mass murderer of Wisconsin, would have repented and given his life to Jesus in prison? I'm glad the wise woman that sent him a Bible correspondence course in prison did it before his fellow prisoner decided to take vengeance into his own hands and murder him.

Your judgment will be like that little firecracker you shot off in the backyard. His will be much more spectacular.

You will be judged for executing judgment. God is perfect, you are not. If you take vengeance into your own hands, you may sin in the process. Then, you are as guilty as your enemy. And you will also be judged by God. "Do not judge, or you too will be judged" (Matthew 7:1).

You have wronged others, right? Do you want that person to judge you, or do you want God to be the judge? Let's practice the Golden Rule here.

When are you supposed to take revenge? NEVER.

In Gene Edwards' book, *A Tale of Three Kings.* he tells the story of Saul, David and Absalom. His theme centers around throwing spears. Saul throws a spear at David. And what does David do? He doesn't throw the spear back. Have you learned that lesson yet? What do you do when someone throws a spear at you? In life there are a lot of spears that will be thrown at you. They may be spears of cutting deeds, but most often the spears are penetrating words. What do you do when these spears are hurled at you? Have you been throwing them back?

If you remember the story, God took care of Saul. God took care of David. And He will take care of you. When someone throws a spear at you, don't throw it back. Never take revenge.

REFLECTING ON LESSON FOUR

1. Who is the typical American hero? Why? How would God's style of hero differ with most media heroes today?

2. What is vengeance? Who does it belong to?

3. When should you take revenge?

4. Why do you want to get revenge so badly?

5. What mistakes are often made concerning revenge?

6. Why shouldn't you take revenge?

7. What would be an example of a Christian vigilante?

8. How have people thrown spears at you in your life? Have you ever thrown them back? If so, how could you have been more like David when Saul threw a spear at him?

5
F I V E

SOMETHING BEAUTIFUL

In 1842, F.W. Robertson, called "the preacher's preacher," started preaching at a church in Cheltenham, England. It was a very wealthy church and a prestigious place to preach. But as the people had become wealthy, they had also become lazy spiritually. But that wasn't the toughest part for Robertson. The church and its leaders had changed and could be characterized by "bitterness, narrowness, and downright meanness."

Robertson's homiletical style was simply preaching through the Bible. As a result, he didn't always own up to traditional interpretations or say things in traditional language. And the liberals of the church said he was too conservative. The conservatives said he was too liberal. They labeled him, libeled him (repeated a lot of stuff about him that at best was secondhand), and even started writing gossip about him in the local newspaper.

This led to what he called his "dark night of the soul." Maybe you have had one of those also. It is the time when you have been wronged, and you take all the emotion to your heart and mind. Then, you try to conclude what to do.

The result of Robertson's dark night was that he turned to the poor and the lower class workers in his city and ministered to them. *The poor didn't care about labels nearly as much as they cared about being loved.* The day he went to the inner city to serve the poor was the day he learned the meaning of Romans 12:21.

"Do not be overcome by evil, but overcome evil with good" (Romans 12:21).

Let's review our steps for overcoming evil:

1. Manage Your Mouth — Bless and Curse Not.

2. See Things From the Other's Point of View (Emotions, Thinking, and Position).

3. Never, Never, Never Take Revenge.

What do you do when someone wrongs you? Usually, we get pretty emotional. As stated earlier, that is when bad relationships generally start. You are emotional and especially sensitive. The other person is emotional and especially insensitive. Isn't that how it happens?

But what is your reaction when you have been wronged? What do you do? Frequently, we stew about it, don't we? And after a good, slow burn, have you become *more* or *less* emotional?

Now, what happens the next time you see this person who has messed up your life? You are real nice and complimentary, right? No! You explode, say something cutting, critical, snub them, avoid them, or curse them! And that really helps, doesn't it? No, it doesn't help at all, and that is why we need our next important point from the text (Romans 12:17b).

The New International Version renders the text this way: "Be careful to do what is right in the eyes of everybody."

> The poor don't care about labels nearly as much as they care about being loved.

However if you read the King James Bible, you will find a different slant: "Provide things honest in the sight of all men."

> **Sit down, think this situation through, get some ideas and come up with a plan.**

What is the best rendering to help us with our dilemma of overcoming evil with good? I got a clue in the New American Standard Bible which reads: "Respect what is right in the sight of all men."

In the side references for the word "respect," it said that it literally meant "take thought for."

As I started studying this word that is translated "provide" or "be careful to do" or "respect," I found out it essentially meant "perceiving beforehand."

In fact, one translation gets right at the heart of this idea from the context of overcoming evil. It reads, "Plan ahead to do what is fine in the sight of all men" (Christian Counselors New Testament).

STEP #4: PLAN AHEAD TO DO SOMETHING BEAUTIFUL.

Analyzing the three parts of this verse in relationship to overcoming evil, we can learn a lot about restoring bad relationships.

PLAN AHEAD

What does it mean to plan ahead? Instead of reacting with your emotions to the person who has wronged you, you are going to plan ahead your response. You know that you are going to see this person again. So instead of reacting and further causing things to fall apart, you are going to *sit down, think this situation through, get some ideas and come up with a plan.*

51

Notice it says "plan ahead." You are supposed to come up with a plan before you ever have the next contact. You think it through. You pray about it. Perhaps you will even get counsel on what would be a good thing to do. You think about the timing. And you create a step by step plan on what you are going to do to overcome this evil.

Remember that we are in a spiritual war. What does any military leader do who is fighting a war? Does he simply march the army along until he meets the enemy? Then based on his emotions of the moment,. he tells the troops what to do. No. He has a plan before the adversary ever attacks.

Notice what Paul says in this passage — "See that none of you repays evil for evil, but always seek to do good to one another and to all" (1 Thessalonians 5:15, NRSV).

Notice here it says to "seek." Don't just do the first thing that comes to your mind. To seek means to look for ways to do something for the person who has wronged you. *You search and you search to find just the right thing to do for this person.*

What are you supposed to plan ahead to do?

TO DO WHAT IS BEAUTIFUL

"Plan ahead to do what is fine in the eyes of every one (Romans 12:17b, Christian Counselors New Testament).

Did you know that you can translate this word for "fine" as "beautiful"? Usually it is translated "good," but here its definition could maybe be seen better as "beautiful." Plan ahead to do something beautiful for this person. *Don't merely settle for the right thing but a beautiful thing to do.*

> You search and you search to find just the right thing to do for this person.

Let's think this through. Suppose

that a person has wronged you. They have lied about you. Maybe, they have taken something that belongs to you. Or they committed adultery against you. What are you supposed to do? Plan out something beautiful to do for them.

The text doesn't tell you what to do. That is because each situation is different. The point is to be creative. Now, you are probably thinking, "You have taken this too far. You can't be serious that I should do something beautiful for the person who has wronged me."

I am saying that this is a radical teaching, seldom practiced, hard to do, and easier to preach than to practice. But yes, I think this is what the Bible is saying.

The reason is because of the cross. When we wronged God, what was the most beautiful thing He could do for us? Knowing our sin, He came up with a plan — the plan of salvation. Jesus would die for our sins, so that He could forgive us. Is anything more beautiful than that plan?

Look at how Paul worded it earlier in Romans.

"You see, at just the right time, when we were still powerless, Christ died for the ungodly Very rarely will anyone die for a righteous man, though for a good man someone might possibly dare to die. But God demonstrates his own love for us in this: While we were still sinners, Christ died for us. Since we have now been justified by his blood, how much more shall we be saved from God's wrath through him!" (Romans 5:6-9).

IN THE SIGHT OF ALL MEN

At first this appears to be confusing. What does Paul mean? Is he telling us to make human standards our model for behavior? No, he is instructing us to do something that is so good that it is irrefutable by everyone.

In other words, your response to the evil done to you should be memorable and convicting to everyone, not just your enemy. Whatever you have planned to do in overcoming evil should be such an act and done in such a manner that skeptics are even compelled to examine your reaction. *Your response should be so profound that it not only moves your enemy to the Lord but also others who observe it.*

Jimmy Carter is a good example of this principle. Probably the greatest compliment that could be said about Jimmy Carter is that most all Republicans say that he is an excellent man. Many of them say he was a poor politician or don't agree with him on issues. But nearly all of his enemies say he is a quality person. His character quiets opponents and makes even his adversaries take notice.

This is the response to the passage. If you are wronged, get a plan. A beautiful plan. A beautiful plan that when you do it, everyone will say, "I can't believe he did that; what a good guy."

Do you know what most of us ought to do today? We ought to think through the situations where we are most likely to blow up, clam up, avoid, say sarcastic or unkind things, and plan out a strategy for what we are going to do the next time we see that person.

> Your response
> should be so
> profound that it
> not only moves
> your enemy to the
> Lord but also
> others who
> observe it.

REFLECTING ON LESSON FIVE

1. Have you ever had a "dark night of the soul"? What caused it?

2. When you are wronged, how do you usually respond emotionally?

3. What is your typical reaction the next time you see the person who wronged you?

4. Why do you need a good plan when you are wronged? What kind of things should be included in your plan?

5. What are some "beautiful" things that could be done to someone you can't stand? How difficult would this be for you?

6. How is the cross the perfect example of a beautiful plan?

7. What does it mean to do something beautiful "in the sight of all men"? Can you give an example of someone who has been recognized for doing this?

8. What strategy or plan do you need to come up with before you meet your bad relationship again?

6

SIX

PEACE — FIGHT FOR IT!

Attending a monthly ministers' meeting had been my habit for years. Most all of us who attended were from the same background and were very comfortable with each other. Many years ago, however, another group of ministers suggested that we all start gathering together. I asked my group if they wanted to start meeting with them. Their response was negative because they thought the other group did some things that were wrong.

As a result, I met with the other ministers over and over again to see if we could reconcile our differences. After much prayer, they decided to give in and do things the way our group did them. Having arrived at unity in practice, I went to our group and said, "You won. Isn't it great that we can now meet together?"

But they said, "No, we still don't want to meet." That's when something dawned on me that I had never noticed before. My group wanted to win the battle, but they didn't want peace. They wanted to prove that the other people were wrong, but they didn't really want a relationship with them. I think that was very wrong, but it is not uncommon.

That's why we need step #5 for overcoming a bad relationship.

> The goal is to have you and your enemy getting along in a good relationship.

STEP #5: DON'T JUST WIN THE WAR, WIN THE PEACE.

Step #5 comes from Romans 12:18.

"If it is possible, as far as it depends on you, live at peace with everyone" (Romans 12:18).

Living at peace is a commandment that Paul gives for our relationships, but it has two qualifiers. In our analysis, let's look at the commandment first and then the two qualifiers.

LIVE AT PEACE WITH EVERYONE

According to Paul, you must do more than win the war against evil. You must also win the peace. Winning a war and winning peace are not always synonymous. But Paul instructs us to triumph in both war and peace.

The battle is not over if peace has not been achieved. Winning the war is insufficient. Just because the conflicts have ended does not mean that you have reached your objective. *The goal is to have you and your enemy getting along in a good relationship.*

Peace doesn't come easily. I'll never forget a bumper sticker that conveyed this idea. It said "Peace — Fight For It."

The writer of Hebrews also recognized the struggle that comes with peacemaking. "Make every effort to live in peace with all men and to be holy; without holiness no one will see the Lord" (Hebrews 12:14).

It takes a great effort to have peace. Even when we are overcoming evil with good, it is possible to have an unhealthy desire for victory. *If we are more glad that they lost than we are happy that good won out, our attitude is somewhat less than Christian.* Our goal is restoration of relationships. Our hope should be that this person who has wronged us will not only end up having a good relationship with us but also with God.

We are trying to turn our adversaries into our allies. Certainly, this is the goal when nations seek peace after engaging in war. How could it be less for personal relationships?

After attending a certain church, it became clear to me that peace wasn't very high on their list of priorities. They fought and argued over everything. You would have thought that "straining at a gnat and swallowing a camel" was how they defined the gospel. If a heated debate wasn't occurring, they thought that they were no longer contending for the faith.

Too many churches don't want things to be peaceful. They are always polarizing over an issue. I once heard it said of a preacher, "He never met a controversy that he didn't like." The critical, faultfinding nature of our society has been owned too often in the church. It is too acceptable today to look for something that you don't like and fight over it. With all the centuries of conflicts over issues that are not the focal point of Christianity, doesn't it make sense that peace would be a good experience in the church?

If we are more glad that they lost than we are happy that good won out, our attitude is somewhat less than Christian.

"Blessed are the peacemakers, for they will be called sons of God" (Matthew 5:9). According to Jesus, you are not going to be happy if you are always fighting. Fighting churches won't be happy churches. By now, we have certainly discovered that bad relationships are not the source of joy.

58

However, this teaching is not only for brothers and sisters in the Lord, but it should also be true for all people. Many of us have become too political. Whether it is arguing about

There are no guarantees here. Peace is not always possible.

the government or religion, we want to fight and prove our side much more than we want to have peace with someone who is different from us. Perhaps Paul gives this first qualifier because he knows that there are some of us who really don't want to get along with others.

IF IT IS POSSIBLE

There are no guarantees here. Peace is not always possible. Now, that doesn't mean that our steps have been incorrect. Let's review our steps.

How to Love Someone You Can't Stand

1. Manage Your Mouth — Bless and Curse Not.

2. See Things from the Other's Point of View (Emotions, Thinking, and Position).

3. Never, Never, Never Take Revenge.

4. Plan Ahead to Do Something Beautiful.

All of these steps are correct and ought to be done. But I can't give you a warranty. There are no absolutes in getting along with people. No matter how hard you try, the end result might not be what you want. You may not win back all your bad relationships.

The struggle against evil can always be won because it is conditional upon God and you. Having peace in your soul is always available for you because it is dependent upon God and you. But having peace with the person who has wronged you depends upon more than God and you. There is a third party, and it's possible that he will reject you no matter how good a person you are.

The methods you use in bringing peace are also restricted. As a Christian, the end doesn't justify the means. Therefore, it may not be possible to do everything that a person who has different values might do to achieve peace. *When peace comes at the expense of biblical compromise, peace is an extravagance that is no longer affordable.*

We must remember the proverb, "When a man's ways are pleasing to the LORD, he makes even his enemies live at peace with him" (Proverbs 16:7).

Did you ever watch the old television series, *Northern Exposure?* This comedic series was filmed in the Northwest where I live. It presented an aspect of life that was very attractive to me, until I started thinking about it. What I liked about *Northern Exposure* was that you have this little town called Cicely that was full of odd and eccentric people. These characters were totally different from each other, and they did all kinds of crazy and absurd stuff like flinging pianos and other large items from a monstrous catapult. But at the end of each episode, all the people got along with each other. I had always liked the way they found a fondness for each other in such diversity. But as I was watching one episode, it dawned on me that a great part of the reason for their harmony was because they tolerated a lot of things that were wrong. As Christians, acceptance of wrongdoing becomes a price that is too high to pay for peace.

When peace comes at the expense of biblical compromise, peace is an extravagance that is no longer affordable.

We Seattleites have been described by other Americans as "Nice." That is the word critics use to best depict us. And it is so nice to be in a nice city. I love living in the city of Seattle. But I've discovered that the reason that we are so nice is because of our tolerance. Our city will accept nearly anything. We just kind of put up with sin. We don't want to say that anything is wrong anymore because then we might not be seen as being nice. In the long run, it may make our city a place that is not a very nice place to live.

The Bible teaches us to hold to God's standards even when others don't like it.

The Bible teaches us to hold to God's standards even when others don't like it. Peace is not to be obtained by compromising God's fundamental truths. That is too great a price.

Going back to your bad relationship, let's assume that you are trying to overcome evil with good. In this process, there may come a time when it seems like everything has been done. This is especially true with a Christian and someone who is not. Very often this happens in marriages where one of the partners is not following the Lord.

A Christian may do their best to have a good relationship with their spouse, but that does not guarantee that the effort will be returned. The Bible acknowledges that this may happen and says — "But if the unbeliever leaves, let him do so. A believing man or woman is not bound in such circumstances; God has called us to live in peace" (1 Corinthians 7:15).

This verse acknowledges that a Christian spouse can do everything to make a good marriage, and their spouse could still leave them. But the text says that even when this is done, it is in the interest of peace.

This verse on marriage should never be isolated from the teaching of Peter who says, "Wives, in the same way be submissive to your husbands so that, if any of them do not believe the word, they may be won over without words by the behavior of their wives, when they see the purity and reverence of your lives" (1 Peter 3:1-2). Peter is giving an excellent example here for how doing good can overcome differences, even in marriage.

Paul is not trying to give an easy out in Romans or First Corinthians for bad relationships. He is simply acknowledging that *you can't make someone else do the right thing just because you have.*

That's why he gives this other qualification:

AS FAR AS IT DEPENDS ON YOU

Your job in a relationship is to do good and seek peace whether the other person does it or not. You are responsible for everything you do in a relationship. But you can't be held accountable if someone else chooses to reject your efforts at reconciliation.

You cannot make a person be at peace with you if they don't want to be.

Let me share with you one of the key philosophies of my life: *You can never get away from God and yourself*

I can get away from you. I can move. I can hide. But wherever I am, there I am. And God is there too.

So *I have to be able to live with God and myself This is fundamental.* I am not going to make it emotionally or spiritually if I can't live with myself . . . or God.

Here's the bottom line. If you do good to a person who has wronged you, one of two things will happen.

1) They will change.

2) They will not change.

It's pretty simple isn't it? If they change, that is what you wanted. If they don't change, at least you can live with yourself and God because you did the right thing.

You can't make someone else do the right thing just because you have.

A huge problem exists if you not only still have a bad relationship, but you are also carrying guilt

62

because you didn't do everything that you could have done. This is especially true in marriages. Be absolutely convinced in the presence of God and facing yourself honestly in the mirror that you have done everything good that you could have done. This doesn't mean

I have to be able to live with God and myself This is fundamental.

that you have been perfect in the relationship. That would be impossible. But it does mean that there is nothing on your conscience now left undone that could still be done.

There is something in being able to say, "I did all that I could do. I haven't left anything undone." When you can make that statement, there is peace. You can live with yourself, and you can live with God.

Have you done all you can do to have peace in this relationship that is eating you up? Or are there some things undone? Can you look in the mirror and say, "I can't think of anything else I can do"? Can you look in the eyes of God and say, "Lord, I have done everything that I know to do. I can't think of anything undone"? If you can, you will have great peace, whether the relationship works out or not.

REFLECTING ON LESSON SIX

1. What is the difference in winning the war and winning the peace? Can you give an example?

2. In what kind of situations do you find it difficult to have peace?

3. How could you have an unholy desire for victory in a relationship even when you were doing the right thing?

4. Have you ever been around a group of Christians who acted like peace wasn't desirable? How was this manifested?

5. In what areas of our lives have we become too political and been fighting too much?

6. Why can't you have peace with everyone?

7. What are areas where we could wrongly compromise in order to have peace?

8. Why is being able to live with God and yourself so important?

9. If you have a bad relationship with someone, have you done all you can do to restore that relationship? What else could you do?

7

S E V E N

RESERVED PARKING

Have you ever taken someone else's parking place? You know it has their name on it. But you just pull in and take it. How do you think that other person feels when they drive up and see someone else's car in their spot? I have a marked parking spot at the college where I teach. One day as I was driving to work, the car in front of me pulled directly into my spot. "Hey, that's my place!" I yelled. "You can't do that!"

Can you imagine doing that with somebody really important? Imagine going someplace like the White House, and there is a spot reserved for "President of the United States." And you just pull in it. I'm sure no one would care. The Secret Service, when they see that it is you, will simply nod and smile.

No, if that spot belongs to someone that important, you would do well to stay out of it. If you want to stay out of trouble, you will find another place to park and leave room for the VIP.

Now, step #3 of overcoming evil with good was "Never, never, never take revenge." That is just like parking in someone else's parking place.

God has reserved the business of vengeance for Himself. It's His parking place.

"Do not take revenge, my friends, but leave room for God's wrath, for it is written: 'It is mine to avenge; I will repay,' says the Lord" (Romans 12:19).

Revenge is not our job. It would be like a secretary sitting at the desk of the C.E.O. and making a few big decisions. Certainly, no one would care, especially not the boss when he returned. You know that's not true!

And yet some of us have tried to sit at God's desk. We have taken his parking place. We act like we are God. It is like we are the judge of what is right and wrong in this world. We decide what is the best thing for ourselves and others to do. We also do this with relationships that go bad. *We think that we really know what went wrong, and we are the only ones who know what should be done.*

STEP #6: MAKE ROOM FOR GOD.

"Leave room," Paul says. In other words, God can really do something in this problem you are facing. Maybe you think it is too bad or too big — but it isn't — for God. Make Him the third party of this relationship.

In the New American Standard Bible, it reads, "Give a place for Him." It is like you are setting the table for you and your enemy, and you make a place for God. If God was personified with you at a table with your enemy, would it change how you behaved? Would you act like you know it all? Would you act like you have everything under control? This would be a pretty good visual exercise, wouldn't it? What would you say and do at that table if God was

We think that we really know what went wrong, and we are the only ones who know what should be done.

sitting there? And you know what? He is.

God is telling you to move over and let Him work.

We crowd God out of our lives, don't we? But it is not simply that we don't give Him our time. It is also that we crowd Him out because we don't think He fits into our high-tech world. He represents that old time religion. It was good for Paul and Silas, but it's not good enough for me. People used to turn to God and pray when they had a problem, or they went to a minister for spiritual counsel. But today we are in a high-tech world where we have become too advanced. I need a scientist, a doctor or a psychotherapist to deal with the complexities of my world. God, He is too simple, too old and outdated. If that is how you have been thinking, your God is too small. God is not outdated. This world is not too complex for God. He is way ahead of us. And He can help.

Paul says "Make room." It is as if someone is coming through that is really big. At the airport the other day, someone yelled at me. "Make room!" they said, because this big electric vehicle was coming right at me. *God is telling you to move over and let Him work.*

We act as if we got ourselves into this mess, so we are going to have to get ourselves out of it. Why don't we let God help? Step aside, make room for God. We act like God doesn't play a role in our lives. Can't God just solve your problem? That might be all that is needed in your particular dilemma. Maybe all that you need to do is simply ask God to do something. God can help in mending broken relationships.

Let me give you three reasons why God can help you with this bad relationship.

GOD JUDGES

"Do not take revenge, my friends, but leave room for God's wrath, for it is written: 'It is mine to avenge; I will repay,' says the Lord" (Romans 12:19).

Remember, we said God repays, not you. In fact as mentioned earlier, that is one of His names — *Yahweh Gmolah*, the Lord of Recompenses. Judgment, that is the name on His parking spot, not yours.

If you are honest, you don't know what your enemy truly deserves. You don't know his heart. You think you do. You are sure that it is bad. But just because this person did you wrong once does not mean that everything about that person is bad.

Your knowledge of the facts is partial. No matter what you think, you don't really know it all. You might give him too much wrath — or too little. (It's possible that he may be worse than you thought.) As individuals, we are not to take revenge. In certain circumstances, God does give limited judgment to the government and the church, but even they cannot judge motives.

The big problem if you were judging me is that you don't know my motives. I can recall situations where I have really wronged some people. And yet when I started out, I had some pretty good motives in my heart. And there have been other times where I have done some pretty nice things with some pretty lousy motives.

God is the only one who can read motives. The writer of Hebrews reminds us of this. "For the word of God is living and active. Sharper than any double-edged sword, it penetrates even to dividing soul and spirit, joints and marrow; it judges the thoughts and attitudes of the

> If you are honest, you don't know what your enemy truly deserves. You don't know his heart.

heart. Nothing in all creation is hidden from God's sight. Everything is uncovered and laid bare before the eyes of him to whom we must give account" (Hebrews 4:12-13).

The only one who can properly judge is the One who sees everything.

> We have a caring relationship with each other because we have a caring relationship with God.

GOD CARES

In our key verse, Paul describes his audience as "friends." He reminds them of the cherished relationships we have in the body of Christ. Christianity is relational. *We have a caring relationship with each other because we have a caring relationship with God.*

Peter sums it up, "Cast all your anxiety on him because he cares for you" (1 Peter 5:7).

Many if not most of our anxieties are rooted in bad relationships. Give them to God. If there is presently someone in your life that you can't stand, give it over to God.

Do you know how to really let your enemy defeat you? First of all, he wrongs you. But *he doubly wins if as a result of his wrong, you allow yourself to get so down that you draw away from God.* Don't let anybody win over you that way. Don't let anyone take you away from God. Haven't you let that happen before?

No matter how much grief this relationship has given you, don't forget that God cares for you. He loves you immensely. He hasn't overlooked the wrongs done to you. He knows that you have been hurt, and He is concerned. Whatever you are feeling, He feels. He cares.

GOD HEALS

As we said, one of the names of God is *Yahweh Gmolah,* the Lord of Vengeance. But let me share with you another one. It has to be one of my favorites — *Yahweh Rapha.* It means the Lord Heals.

We are going to discover the use of the name of *Yahweh Rapha* in Exodus 15. Israel had been delivered by the Lord's hand from their long enslavement in Egypt. Having been delivered from Pharaoh and from death by the Passover Lamb, don't you know they felt free? When they got to the Red Sea and Yahweh parted those waters, don't you think they were saying, "Now we have left all of our troubles behind"?

But no sooner had they sung their song of celebration, than they started wondering if they were going to die of thirst. The Red Sea was too salty, and they came to Marah and it was bitter. They started wondering if they were going to die. They cried out, "What shall we drink?" So Moses calls out to *Yahweh Yireh* (the Lord Who Provides).

"Then Moses cried out to the LORD, and the LORD showed him a piece of wood. He threw it into the water, and the water became sweet. There the LORD made a decree and a law for them, and there he tested them. He said, 'If you listen carefully to the voice of the LORD your God and do what is right in his eyes, if you pay attention to his commands and keep all his decrees, I will not bring on you any of the diseases I brought on the Egyptians, for I am the LORD, who heals you'" (Exodus 15:25-26).

Your enemy wins doubly if as a result of his wrong, you allow yourself to get so down that you draw away from God.

Did you notice how God describes Himself in verse 26? He reveals Himself as *Yahweh Rapha,* the Lord who heals. He is the God who makes their bitter waters sweet and leads

70

them to the Promised Land. But can't our God still make bitter waters sweet? Yes, He can heal you today.

Yahweh Rapha heals. What does He heal? He heals physically — our sicknesses. I believe that. That's why we pray for people when they are sick.

Yahweh Rapha heals spiritually. That's why we pray for people when they are entrapped in sin.

But I also believe *Yahweh Rapha* is the healer of broken relationships. No matter what it is — whether it is a threatening divorce, a big fight at church, or a major squabble in the office — you need to make room for God.

He is the healer of broken relationships.

But *Yahweh Rapha* heals more than a broken relationship. He heals *you*. "He heals the brokenhearted and binds up their wounds" (Psalm 147:3).

When your heart is broken, He can heal it.

When a relationship is broken, it is more than the relationship that is broken. You are broken. And when you are broken, who can put you back together again? Who can heal? It is *Yahweh Rapha*. He heals all of your diseases. But more than that — it says He heals *you!* (Exodus 15:26). He is the only one who can heal you in this broken relationship.

Our conclusion in the previous chapter was that one of two things happens in a bad relationship when we do good. Our enemy changes, or he doesn't change.

But even if that person who wrongs you doesn't change, you can change. You will change for the better if you overcome with good. God is working even in your bad relationships to change you. And in the process, He heals you. When the Great Physician works, it is like many of the doctors that I know today. Their methods of healing hurt a little bit.

In a counseling situation recently, I was telling my friend how he ought to do something good to the person who had really wronged him at work. And he responded and said, "Then that guy will win. He will get what he really wanted." And in one sense he was right. It would appear to everyone that his enemy had won.

But *being the winner in everyone else's eyes is not the decisive factor for relationships.* Therefore I told him, "You will not lose by doing the right thing because you will walk away a bigger and better man. I will know that you did the right thing, and you will be a winner with me. But more than that, you will know and God will know. And that is what really matters. So indeed you will be the real winner."

There is an internal victory that happens to you when you do good. And I don't want you to miss it.

Moses Lard in his commentary on this passage stated, "By this course, you will certainly conquer the evil which is in yourself, and you may conquer that which is in him."

Though you may not cease to make a person an enemy in the sense of one who hates you, you can make a person not an enemy in the sense of one who is hated. Is he your enemy because he hates you or because you hate him? He may still hate you, but when you do good, maybe you will lose your hatred.

Being the winner in everyone else's eyes is not the decisive factor for relationships.

Paul is teaching us that if your enemy doesn't change by doing good, at least you do.

God can be the total difference in a bad relationship. So make room for Him.

REFLECTING ON LESSON SEVEN

1. In a previous bad relationship, how have you taken God's role and "parked in His spot"?

2. What picture comes to your mind when the Bible teaches us to "leave room" for God?

3. Why do most people crowd God out of their lives today?

4. What are the characteristics of God that help mend broken relationships?

5. What makes God a better judge than yourself?

6. How has God demonstrated His care for you in a tough relationship?

7. How does God heal in a relationship? Has He ever healed you? Tell your story.

8. Have you ever changed by doing good even when a relationship didn't change? How did this happen?

8
E I G H T

DROPPING THE BIG ONE

The story of the defense of Masada is a dramatic and tragic tale of a few Jewish families who held off a huge Roman army in the middle of the Judean desert.

How in the world could they do it? It really wasn't as difficult as it might seem. They simply had positioned themselves on the top of a huge rock mountain near the Dead Sea. There were only a couple of little paths that snaked up the side of the mountain, and they were only wide enough for one person. Any time someone would try to get up to the fortress, the Jewish people merely dropped objects from above which stopped their enemies dead in their tracks. If you go there today, you can still see some of the old rocks they used to drop nearly two thousand years ago. Most of us would consider ourselves too civilized to drop rocks on our enemies' heads, yet the Bible tells us to do something that sounds nearly as bad. Romans 12 tells us to heap burning coals on our enemies' heads!

Who are your enemies? We usually don't call people "enemies" today. No, we tend to call them "bad relationships."

Most of us don't have to look very far to find a bad relationship. And what is most surprising is where we find them. In fact, most often bad relationships are very close to home. Yes, we can have enemies at home, work, school, with our neighbors and even at church.

If you are tired of soured relationships, the seven steps from Romans 12 will give you a way to overcome them. It will not necessarily repair all of them, but it is a way to win over them. At least we no longer have to let bad relationships destroy our lives. But *God's way for overcoming an evil done to you is so radical that you may still doubt that it will work* or even be hesitant to try it. Yet, it is still God's way.

How do you overcome a bad relationship? You do good to your enemy. No matter how many times we examine this text, it is still revolutionary.

"Do not be overcome by evil, but overcome evil with good" (Romans 12:21).

When we are wronged by someone, certainly we feel like the person who harmed us deserves the very worst. But the Bible tells us that we are to respond with good. And according to God this is the best way to end a bad relationship. Do good.

Our main text to lead us to Step #7 is Romans 12:20.

"On the contrary: 'If your enemy is hungry, feed him; if he is thirsty give him something to drink. In doing this, you will heap burning coals on his head'" (Romans 12:20).

STEP #7: BOMB PEOPLE WITH LOVE.

Years ago, a member of the congregation where I preach waited to be the last person to talk to me every Sunday morning. Week after week, he would tell me how bad everything was at church, especially the preacher. Needless to say, it bothered me. As I drove home from church, even though other people had given me positive feedback, I would be haunted by his evaluation.

His negativism nearly made me want to quit. Instead, I decided to do something different. No longer would I wait for him to talk to me. I started initiating the conversations. Barbie and I frequently invited him to eat with us. In fact, we befriended him. We decided to go overboard in our response to him. Everything nice that we could possibly think of doing for him, we did.

What I discovered in the process was that he was a very lonely person. His criticism was actually a cry for love. What he had done was wrong, but it became more understandable as we came to know him. He no longer lives in Seattle, but by the time he left here, he would have probably called me his best friend, and his favorite preacher.

Our passage for Step #7 tells us how to go about this process. Doing good involves a three-step method.

FIND A NEED

Analyze the situation. In this case, the enemy is identified as hungry or thirsty If that is the case, feed him or give him something to drink.

Everyone has a need of some kind. Find out what it is.

Now, your enemy may not be lacking food or water, but *everyone has a need of some kind. Find out what it is.* It may take time and effort to discover what is lacking in their life.

76

Don't just guess or assume their needs are the same as yours. What is so beneficial about this whole process is that it takes the focus off of yourself. It helps you to understand what another person is like. When you see the world from their shoes, it will be easier to have a relationship with them.

> I don't think that there is a person on this planet who isn't walking around hoping that someone will love them.

And if you are still having trouble figuring your enemy out, just remember — everybody has the need to be loved. *I don't think that there is a person on this planet who isn't walking around hoping that someone will love them.* If someone had shown your enemy some love in the first place, perhaps they would have never harmed you as they did.

LOOK AT YOUR RESOURCES

What do you have to give? When God saw our need, he looked at His resources and gave us what we most needed — His Son.

Take an inventory of your resources. Look at your funds, your possessions, your time, your life. See what you have that can meet their needs. This goes back to Step #4 where we learned the principle of planning ahead to do something beautiful in a relationship.

HEAP GOOD

Finally, *if you are going to win over your enemy, you have to do something.* There must be words. Step #1 tells us to "Bless and curse not." But words are not enough. There must be action.

And one little thing may not be enough. Doing good is described as heaping coals. Heaping means a lot. You drop the big bomb of love on them. You will probably have to do a lot of good to win over a bad relationship. If your marriage is a battleground, one small thing will not overcome an estranged relationship. Husbands, did you hear that? If you have a bad relationship with your wife, it may take a little more than bringing her flowers one time.

What is the result of doing all of this good? You will heap burning coals on your enemy.

That sounds a lot like vengeance, but it is not.

Jay Adams in his book, *How to Overcome Evil*, states: "There is no thought of punishment here . . . Your goal is to overcome his evil with your good. The coals are your good deeds heaped on him. Remember, Paul has warfare in mind. In his day, they didn't have flame throwers, but they knew that fire was an effective weapon.

"If you could get coals (of smokeless undetectable charcoal, as the word here indicates) on your enemy's head, you would effectively put him out of business as an enemy. You would subdue and overcome him."

Opinions about the meaning of "burning coals" have been very diverse. One view is that it represents God's simmering judgment. This interpretation fits well with the passage in Psalm 140.

"Let the heads of those who surround me be covered with the trouble their lips have caused. Let burning coals fall upon them; may they be thrown into the fire, into miry pits, never to rise" (Psalm 140:9-10).

If you are going to win over your enemy, you have to do something.

Another theory believes this is a reference to the ancient Bedouin sign of homage where hot coals are given to someone who has no fire.

Dr. Dan Allender in his book, *Bold Love*, says it is referring to shame.

78

This view fits the essence of the passage. When you have been doing really bad things to someone and they come right back and love you, don't you just feel ashamed of yourself? All of us do. We feel like someone just dropped a bomb on us.

> Goodness has the power to expose and shame the one who did harm.

Dr. Allender states, "Evil cannot tolerate the intrusion of goodness. Evil has its own snarl, dress code, favorite beer, and sports team, and when someone comes into its lair sporting a smile, out of fashion wide lapels, and a root beer, it can hardly bear to coexist with this alien and stranger. It depends on its ability to mock and shame the intruder into retreat. . . . In other words *goodness has the power to expose and shame the one who did harm.* Shame is the experience of having the curtain lifted and being recognized as the wizard of a sham kingdom. . . . For that reason, I understand the metaphor of 'heaping burning coals on the head' to mean offering goodness that surprises, supplants and shames the sin of the one who does harm, lest it remain and destroy his heart. Shame can be a severe mercy, a gift of sight that either hardens or softens the heart."

Shame will always cause a person to change. It will either cause the intensity of the evil to heighten, or it will soften a person's heart.

But isn't this process of heaping coals simply another way to make people feel guilty? No. You are trying to do good. Your enemy is already guilty if they have wronged you. Good may make them realize how they are and make them want to change.

Feeling guilty when we are guilty is not bad.

Guilt is what we feel when we first realize our own sinfulness in the sight of God's grace. Are we ruined by that guilt? Some are. But others recognize that the whole point of feeling guilty was to motivate us to a good relationship. God wants to forgive us and have a good relationship with us. As Paul mentions earlier in Romans, "Or do you show contempt for the riches of his kindness, tolerance and patience, not realizing that God's kindness leads you toward repentance?" (Romans 2:4).

Doing good may produce a guilt that leads to grace. When you do good, you don't do it for revenge, but out of grace (giving what someone doesn't deserve). A gift of grace is always accompanied by a willingness to forgive.

If your good works are not linked to graciousness, the bad relationship may not be healed even though you exhibited good works. It is true that they wronged you, and they deserve bad. But if you are not willing to forgive them, all of the doing of good will have been done in vain. Many want their enemies to be shamed but do not really have the desire to forgive them. Having their heads burn is the *result* of doing good, not the motivation for doing it.

There is nothing that feels much better than forgiveness. Sure, it is tough at first to forgive someone who has wronged you. It is difficult to imagine trying to like that person you can't stand. But once that grace is extended and is accepted, walls come down. And you will feel much better with a restored relationship. Bad relationships carry a lot of stress and negative energy around with them. Forgiveness will make you feel better physically, psychologically, and spiritually.

If your good works are not linked to graciousness, the bad relationship may not be healed.

I'm wondering if you don't need to feel good today Practice these principles from Romans 12. They are tough, but I promise they will work. Try these seven steps. If there is someone you can't stand, I think you can stand to do them.

REFLECTING ON LESSON EIGHT

1. Where do most of your bad relationships occur?

2. What are common needs that most of your enemies have?

3. What resources do you have to offer people who wrong you?

4. What would be an example of "heaping" good upon someone?

5. What is the meaning of Paul's "burning coals" illustration?

6. Have you ever felt ashamed when someone responded with good to you when you were not nearly so gracious to them? Tell your story.

7. How does shame cause a person to change?

8. Has there ever been a time when you wanted to see a person shamed but you really didn't want to forgive them? Explain.

9. How are guilt and grace connected?

10. Have you ever felt the wonderful feeling of forgiving someone you can't stand? What would it take for you to experience that feeling again with a current bad relationship?

About the Author

Milton Jones has served as preaching minister with the Northwest Church of Christ in Seattle, Washington since 1978. Dr. Jones is also a professor of preaching and evangelism at Puget Sound Christian College. He is senior editor of *Campus Crosswalk* and outreach editor of *21st Century Christian.* His previous books include *Grace: the Heart of the Fire* and *Discipling: the Multiplying Ministry.* Milton and his wife, Barbie, have two sons, Pat and Jeremy.

ALSO FROM THIS AUTHOR. . .

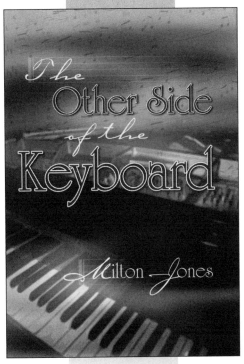

The Other Side of the Keyboard

Milton Jones

The Other Side of the Keyboard: What does that mean? The keyboard is the instrument that separates two distinct fellowships—the Churches of Christ and the Christian Churches. No one expects people who read this book to leave their instruments and sing only a cappella music. Nor is anyone trying to coerce others to use musical instruments. This new book was not written to argue with anyone, but in hopes that each side would learn something about the other. No matter what your predisposition, Milt Jones is on your side, as long as it's the side of the cross.

64 pages, soft, G07-918-2
$6.99

To order call 1.800.289.3300 or visit our
website at www.collegepress.com

Shepherding evokes idyllic images of green pastures, fluffy sheep, and carefree shepherds lou[...] in the grass. But shepherding is not all lazy days spent by a babbling brook. Shepherding i[...] hard work; in fact it can be downright demanding.

It is in these images that God chose to communicate not only how He cares for us, but also how [...] leaders are to care for the church.

We are very excited to unveil a new series in 2007. As you minister to your congregation, you wi[...] situations that stretch and challenge you. The Caring for the Flock series is designed to help you ac[...] the needs and concerns every shepherd faces. If you would like more information about this series, or if you would like to receive notification of new re[...] within this series please visit www.collegepress.com and click on the Caring for the Flock link or call 1-800-289-3300.

A Shepherd's Guide to Counseling Fundamentals
Beth Robinson

While individuals frequently seek out ministers to assist with counseling issues, many ministers have limited tr[...] about counseling strategies and techniques. *A Shepherd's Guide to Counseling Fundamentals* was written to help ministers to respond to the counseling needs of the members of the congregation in a godly and effective manner.

Table of Contents:
**On the Front Line • Stages of the Counseling Process • The Counseling Relation[...]
Understanding Crisis Intervention • Understanding Life Transitions
Understanding Relationship Problems • Understanding Mental Illness
What Now?**

Beth Robinson teaches at Lubbock Christian University in Lubbock, Texas, where she leads the Departme[...] Behavioral Sciences. She is a licensed professional counselor, an approved supervisor for licensed professional couns[...] and a certified school counselor. Beth's simple yet engaging writing syle makes this an excellent resource for any[...] istry professional in need of a quick reference guide for counseling basics.
90 pages, soft, #CF07-694-9, $8.99

Four Marks of the Healthy Ministry Professional
John W. Daniels, III & Daniel S. Yearick

The shepherd must take care of himself to be able to take care of the sheep. This book addresses the disturbing fact that the success of those in the ministry often comes at the expense of the person God created them to be. We not only expect our ministers to meet our expectations, but often demand that they meet those expectations in exactly the way we want them to be met. *Four Marks of the Healthy Ministry Professional* will help you ask the right questions that will guide you to wholeness.

Table of Contents:
**Introduction • The Burden of Unresolved Issues
A Destorted View of "Call" • Boundaries • Friendship
A Life and Ministry of Integrity • Conclusion**

John Daniels serves as Associate Pastor for Christian Formation and Administration at First Baptist Church, Waynesville, North Carolina. He is a graduate of Carson Newman College where he earned a bachelor's degree in Religion, and also holds a master's degree in Religious Education from Southwestern Baptist Theologicial Seminary.

Dan Yearick is a licensed professional counselor. He holds a bachelor's degree in Social Work from Roberts Wesleyan College and a master's degree in Counselor Education from The State University of New York, College at Brockport. He currently maintains a private counseling practice in Waynesville, North Carolina.
95 pages, soft, #CF07-926-1, $8.99

To order call 1.800.289.3300 or
visit our website at
www.collegepress.com